ADRENAL FATIGUE

Why am I so tired all the time?

Holly Fourchalk, PhD., DNM®, RHT, HT

CHOICES UNLIMITED
FOR
HEALTH & WELLNESS

This book includes neither an exhaustive nor exclusive list of alternative options for working with adrenal fatigue.

Rather, it provides an overview of theories, foods, herbs and modalities with which the patient or practitioner may work.

My company is called Choices Unlimited for Health and Wellness for a reason. There are lots of choices to choose from with regard to maximizing your health. We can only make good, effective choices when we have a working knowledge of what those choices may be.

If a given modality or protocol resonates for you, research it further. Explore your options within the profile. Your mind is a very powerful tool – make it work for you. Regardless of what you choose to do, make the placebo effect – or the power of the mind – be a part of your healing journey.

Here's to your journey into health.

DISCLAIMER

Every effort has been made by the author to ensure that the information in this book is as accurate as possible. However, it is by no means a complete or exhaustive examination of all information.

The author knows what worked for her and what has worked for others but no two people are the same and so the author cannot and does not render judgment or advice regarding a particular individual.

Further, because our bodies are unique any two individuals may experience different results from the same therapy.

The author believes in both prevention and the superiority of a natural non-invasive approach over drugs and surgery.

The information collected within comes from a variety of researchers and sources from around the world. This information has been accumulated in the Western healing arts over the past thirty years.

Research has shown that one of the top three leading causes of death in North America oc-curs because of the physician/pharmaceutical component of the scenario.

Perhaps the real leading cause of death and disability is a result of the lack of awareness of natural therapies. These therapies are well known to prevent and treat many common degenerative, inflammatory and oxidative diseases.

The author loves to research and loves to teach. This book is another attempt to increase awareness about health and the many options we have to bring the body back into a healthy balance.

Ever-increasing numbers of people are aware of healing foods and herbs, supplements and modalities but there are still far too many who are not. The fact that our physicians are part of this latter group makes healing even more challenging yet we are now seeing more and more laboratories around the world and more universities in and outside of the U.S. studying herbs, nutrition and various healing modalities with phenomenal success.

The unfortunate fact is, those who can profit from sickness and disease promote ignorance and the results are devastating.

It is not the intent of the author that anyone

should choose to read this book and make decisions regarding their health or medical care based on ideas contained in this book.

It is the responsibility of the individual to find a health care practitioner to work with to achieve optimal health.

The author and publisher are not responsible for any adverse effects or consequences resulting from the use of any of the suggestions or information contained in the book but offer this material as information that the public has a right to hear and utilize at its own discretion.

To my Parents

For all their support and encouragement
My Dad for his ever-listening ear
My mother for her open mind

ADRENAL FATIGUE

CONTENTS

ONE

Why do we need to bother with the adrenals?

Are you one of the suspected 80% of population in the western world that suffers with adrenal issues?

You may be, yet you may not even suspect that you have a problem. Do you drift through life in a haze, simply accepting that you:

- Don't sleep well?
- Have low periods in the afternoon?
- Wake up tired?
- Don't have a lot of get up and go?
-

Are you one of those people who runs on adrenaline? Do you feel:

- Burnt out?
- Stressed out?
- Worn out?
- Tired?
- Frustrated?

But you keep going anyway?

Do you keep going because?

- You need the finances?
- You are a single parent with children to support?
- You are developing a new career and putting everything you have into it?
- You are afraid of losing your job?

There are all kinds of reasons people keep pushing themselves and keep going beyond what is healthy. But what is going on in their bodies? And how long can they continue before they crash?

The adrenals are meant to kick in primarily in a flight or fight situation. They are designed to put out the necessary hormones in a big way for a short period of time but to recover they require significant downtown time – days, or even weeks.

In Western society, we have learned to rely on our adrenal glands to keep going. We don't take the time we need to relax and recover. The two days a week wherein we squeeze all our chores is not sufficient time for the adrenals to recover from the strain of daily living.

Further, the adrenals jump into action not only with psychological stress but also with gut stress. We all know how stressed our gut is in response to the North American diet, don't we? Consequently, we have very stressed, overworked adrenals.

The adrenals are responsible for a lot more than just reacting to stress but when overwhelmed from responding to stress, all the other functions get compromised as well. This creates a whole series of resulting problems.

So, how do we know if we have adrenal fatigue and what do we do about it if we have it?

Let's start with understanding the adrenals first then we will look at how they respond to both gut and psychological stress. We will look at the symptoms and other resulting or causative health issues then finally, what we can do to care of the adrenal glands.

TWO

What are the adrenals and what do they do?

Adrenal is a Latin word combined from two components:

- Ad – Latin for near
- Renes – Latin for kidneys

That makes sense since the adrenals are two little glands that sit on top of the kidneys. Interestingly, these two small hormonal glands are shaped differently from each other. The one on the left is a semilunar-shaped gland, while the one on the right is more of a triangular shaped-gland.

Adrenal Gland

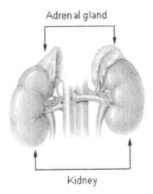

The glands weigh approximately 3-5 grams each. They are divided into two distinct components: the interior component or the medulla, and the exterior component, or the cortex.

Right Adrenal Gland   Left Adrenal Gland

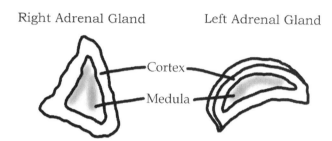

These two glands are vitally important for a number of functions. Most people, however, are familiar only with the stress reaction, or the fight flight response, in which the adrenals are involved. In this kind of situation, they release epinephrine and norepinephrine, otherwise known as, adrenaline and noradrenaline.

However, the adrenal glands are involved in a variety of other functions as well.

The adrenal *cortex*, or outside portion of the gland is regulated by hormones secreted from the pituitary gland in the brain, which in turn is regulated by the hypothalamus in the brain. Consequently, we have what is called the hypothalamus-pituitary-adrenal axis (HPA).

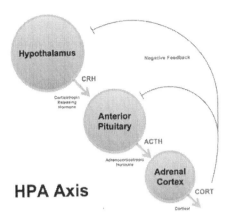

HPA Axis

The hypothalamus, a primary regulating organ in the brain, releases CRH (corticotrophin) releasing hormone that stimulates the pituitary to release ACTH (adrenocorticotrophic hormone) that in turn stimulates the adrenals to release cortisol.

Cortisol plays a role in:

- Regulating blood sugar
- Suppressing the immune system
- Aiding in fat metabolism
- Aiding in protein metabolism
- Aiding in carbohydrate metabolism
- Regulating inflammation

The interactions between these organs in the HPA (Hypothalamus – Pituitary - Adrenal axis) and the resulting production of substances control such functions as:

- Digestion
- Energy storage and expenditure
- Immune system
- Mood and emotions
- Reactions to stress
- Sexuality
- Various other body processes

The adrenal *cortex* has three different layers of cells that are organized to produce different substances:

- The outer layer (Zona glomerulosa):
  - Mineralocorticoids (predominantly aldosterone)
- The middle layer (Zona fasciculate):
  - Glucocorticoids (predominantly cortisol)
- The inside layer (Zona reticularis)
  - Androgens (predominantly DHEA and testosterone)

The adrenal *medulla*, or the inside core, on the other hand, secretes predominantly catecholamines:

- Adrenaline (epinephrine = 80%)
- Noradrenaline (norepinephrine = 20%)

These are the fight-flight hormones with which people are most often familiar.

The medulla is regulated through the sympathetic nervous system and releases hormones directly into the blood.

Three different blood arteries supply nutrients to the adrenal glands. Toxins are removed and hormones are secreted through the suprarenal veins, which disperse differently on each side of the body.

As one studies the adrenals, it becomes more and more apparent that these two tiny glands can have an enormous impact on the body and in a variety of different ways.

Let's now look at the adrenals and see what kinds of problems they can encounter, what causes them, how we can know if we have these problems and how to address them.

THREE

Adrenal Disorders

While this book is focused largely on the disorder known as adrenal fatigue, there are a number of other disorders that can affect the adrenal glands. When the adrenals are either over-functioning or under-functioning, they cause problems.

In addition, a number of different issues can cause over- or under-functioning of the adrenals, including:

- **Tumors:** depending on the location and consistency of the tumor, it may provoke over- or under-functioning of the adrenals.
- **Hyperaldosteronism:** the name given when the adrenals produce too much aldosterone.
- **Pheochromocytoma:** the name given when the adrenals produce excessive amounts of catecholamines.
- **Cushing's syndrome:** the name given when the adrenals produce too much cortisol – this is the condition that usually precedes adrenal fatigue.

- **Adrenal insufficiency**: the name given when the adrenals produce insufficient amounts of cortisol or aldosterone. This may be due to issues in the adrenals *or* the pituitary *or* the hypothalamus.
  - **Addison's disease**: the name given when the adrenals produce insufficient glucocorticoids, especially cortisol (may be due to an auto-immune reaction, infection, depleted levels of ACTH or depleted levels of glutathione).
  - **Congenital adrenal hyperplasias:** name given to genetic defects of enzymes involved in the production of cortisol and sex hormones.
  - **Waterhouse-friderichsen syndrome**: name that identifies the cause of adrenal production which is caused by the severe bacterial infection.
  - **Adrenal fatigue**: when the adrenals function below the necessary level.

Adrenal fatigue has a historical dance of different names:

- Non-Addison's hypoadrenia

- Sub-Clinical hypoadrenia
- Neurasthenia
- Adrenal neurasthenia
- Adrenal apathy

And now today: Adrenal fatigue.

The challenge with adrenal fatigue is that like many disorders and dysfunctions, Western medicine lags behind medical science. This was also the case with:

- Chronic Fatigue Syndrome
- Fibromyalgia
- Leaky Gut Syndrome
- Eating Disorders

Many claim that adrenal fatigue affects millions of people but these cases go undiagnosed because conventional medicine does not recognize the disorder. Dr. John Tinterra, a medical doctor who specialized in low adrenal function, estimated that approximately 16% of the public could be classified as suffering from severe adrenal fatigue but that if all indications of low cortisol were included, the percentage would be more like 66%.

See:
http://www.adrenalfatigue.org/what-is-

adrenal-fatigue#what-is-adrenal-fatigue

Adrenal fatigue usually follows a prolonged period of stress and heightened adrenal output. This may be due to:

- Cognitive stress
- Emotional stress
- Immune stress: acute or chronic

The challenge with adrenal fatigue is that the symptoms typically appear slowly and do not show any particular outward sign, such as a rash.

Adrenal fatigue can have a massive impact on your life because of the symptoms, which may include:

- Fatigue not relieved by sleep
- Inability to get out of bed or to stay up for more than a few hours
- Changes in metabolism of:
    - Carbohydrates
    - Proteins
    - Fat
- Changes in the regulation of:
    - Electrolytes
    - Fluids
    - Heart & vascular function
    - Sex drive

As a subsequence of the above issues, other biological dysfunctions may evolve, not only at the systems and organ level but also at the cellular level.

As already noted, hormones regulate all the different systems in the body. Hormones act as the messengers between the different systems and organs in the body. When these hormones are out of balance, the body's capacity to function becomes compromised. If this is not taken care of, a domino effect ensues.

Unfortunately, this domino effect goes unnoticed until something dramatic happens.

Consequently, by the time people get to the point where they are willing to invoke some help, they have incurred a variety of issues. The MDs then prescribe medications that simply attempt to manage the symptoms. While alternative health practitioners may attempt to resolve the underlying issues, all too often the sufferer is too impatient to address all of the accompanying problems that were created along the way to adrenal fatigue.

FOUR

Adrenal Fatigue – Cognitive Stress

Cognitive stresses can be very challenging because often they are mixed in with emotional stresses. For most people, it is difficult to have one kind of stress without the other.

Very simply, a cognitive stressor is one that causes an unwanted reaction. However, these reactions can very widely from one person to another.

We all know that *different* people interpret *different* situations *differently*. Consequently, when a particular situation occurs, any given person may have one of a variety of different interpretations:

- Guilt
- Shame
- Fear
- With responsibility
- As an opportunity

Obviously, how we interpret a given situation is going to determine how we choose to respond to it but even the *reaction* to a given interpretation may be different between different people. A variety of people will respond to the same situation differently. For instance, any one person may:

- Avoid
- Deny
- Run away
- Address the issue
- Attack the issue
- Manoeuvre around the issue.

In addition to the above factors, we can also have underlying life themes that we may not even by conscious of that impact how we interpret or respond to the world. For instance, you can certainly understand how a person who has a strong underlying sense of *inadequacy* is going to interpret and respond to the world in a very different way than the person who is *narcissistic* or thinks he is better than everyone else.

Another type of cognitive stress is when we operate against our beliefs, our morals or our values. When we are not behaving in "sync" with our own system, this too will cause stress.

Consequently, what might be a cognitive stressor for one person may not be a stressor at all for another person. Because of this, we cannot hope to give a simple black and white definition of what a cognitive stressor is.

What we can say is that, if your thoughts are causing you stress, then they will have an impact on your adrenals.

FIVE

Adrenal Fatigue – Emotional Stress

Emotional stress can be provoked by a wide variety of issues in life. This may be the result of, or intertwined with, our ongoing thoughts. It may also be the result of situations we feel we have no control over or no say in.

We may also have emotions that don't even seem to be attached to anything in particular. For instance, generalized fear or anxiety refers to the emotional experience when there is no apparent reason for it.

In today's society, we all have a wide variety of emotional stresses that we live with and have to cope with or manage.

Two of the most common issues for people today are toxic relationships and trouble with finances. Because the results of these two factors penetrate through much of our lives, today's families have a lot on their plates. Consequently, the family structure is challenged both from the outside and from the inside.

When people are challenged financially, they

carry the stress of it 24/7. Because of financial stress people:

- Stay in jobs they hate
- Work in environments that are toxic and abusive
- Carry the load of it home with them.

People also stay in toxic relationships for a wide variety of reasons believing:

- This too will pass
- He/she really does love me
- I have to stay for the children
- And many more reasons…

In addition to financial problems, toxic relationships and divorce, families may have to deal with other sources of emotional stress. Families suffer greatly when they have lost a child or a partner through:

- Illness
- Accidents
- War

The loss of a child or a partner, regardless of the reason, is considered one of the most challenging stresses on any family.

All of these stressors have an impact on the adrenals. Initially, our adrenals may go into overdrive, struggling to help us to keep going but eventually they may crash and simply not be able to keep up with the demands put on them.

SIX

Adrenal Fatigue – Gut Stress

People usually think of themselves as having only one brain, when in fact, the gut is considered the second brain. In fact, the gut produces more neurotransmitters than the brain does. The gut and the adrenals work together.

You will remember from Chapter Two, that CRF released from the hypothalamus stimulates the pituitary to release ACTH, which in turn stimulates the adrenals to release cortisol.

However, we also know that receptors for the CRF substance are also found in gut. Consequently, stress can result in changes in the:

- Transport of stool or intestinal motility
- Gut sensitivity
- Gut inflammation
- Gut immune system

These issues may be experienced as:

- Constipation

- Abdominal Pain
- Abdominal Cramps
- Abdominal Bloating

Another important problem is gut permeability. The gut is a long continuous tube that runs from the mouth to the anus. Different parts of the intestinal tube are lined with different tissues that produce different substances, require a different pH (acidity or alkalinity) and support different bacteria. The hundreds of bacteria that are found throughout the intestines perform a variety of different jobs metabolizing the nutrients we ingest.

The cells that line this tube are held tightly together to protect the body from what is in the gut *and* to regulate the substances that are metabolized, absorbed or eliminated.

The resulting domino effects of stress can loosen the gut's ability to protect and regulate the substances within it, which then causes it to become compromised. This person now has what is called "leaky gut syndrome".

Because 90% of the immune system is in the gut, the immune system starts to identify these substances (What substances? Food?) as "antigens" and creates an immune response against them. Unfortunately, this can be the beginning of auto-immune disorders.

The inflammatory response system kicks in and also starts to provoke other problems like:

- Abdominal bloating
- Depression
- Fatigue
- Foggy thinking
- Food allergies
- Hay fever
- Indigestion
- Joint pain
- Mood swings
- Skin rashes

There are other problems with the gut that interact with the adrenals. For instance, previously we noted that glutathione was the body's primary chelator: meaning it draws toxic metals out of the blood and gut.

If glutathione levels are low (which prevents the pituitary from making ACTH), toxic metals will also start to build up then we can have a whole paradigm of other issues to contend with.

Toxic metals have an enormous impact on our entire system. For instance, the following is a list of some of the symptoms from lead toxicity:

- Insomnia
- Cognitive deficits
- Tremor
- Hallucinations
- Convulsions

Or aluminum toxicity:

- Muscle weakness
- Bone pain
- Fractures that do not heal, especially in ribs and pelvis
- Cognitive impairment
- Premature Osteoporosis
- Anemia
- Impaired iron absorption
- Impaired immunity
- Seizures
- Dementia
- Growth retardation in children
- Spinal deformities: Scoliosis or kyphosis

It is important to eliminate any and all metal toxicities from the body. Thus, it is important to get our glutathione levels up.

SEVEN

Symptoms of Adrenal Fatigue

Wow, this is going to be a challenging chapter.

Many people go around with undiagnosed adrenal fatigue symptoms simply because the symptoms can be so diverse. To help you understand all this, I have provided both a short list and a long list of possible symptoms.

The short list consists of the most common, well recognized symptoms. If you are experiencing one or more of the following, you may be experiencing adrenal fatigue:

- You crave salty and sweet snacks
- You feel tired for no reason
- You repeatedly wake up tired even if you had a good night's sleep
- You feel rundown and/or overwhelmed
- You have difficulty recovering from stress or illness
- Fatigue
- You feel more awake, alert and energetic after 6 p.m. than you do all day.

Now let's look at the longer list, which in

addition to the above includes:

- Oversensitivity to bright sunlight – sodium-potassium imbalance
- Muscle weakness
- Bald patches on your arms or legs
- Hollow cheeks
- Pale lips
- Vertical lines in the skin on the fingertips
- Inability to recover effectively from exercise (20-30 minute recovery time)
- Headaches with physical or mental stress
- Weak immune system and allergies
- Slow to start in the morning
- Gastric ulcers
- Afternoon headaches
- Feeling full or bloated
- Craving sweets, caffeine or cigarettes
- Blurred vision
- Unstable behavior
- Becoming shaky or light-headed if meals are missed or delayed
- Cannot stay asleep or cannot fall asleep
- Dizziness when moving from sitting to standing or lying to standing
- Transient spells of dizziness
- Asthma
- Hemorrhoids, varicose veins

A well utilized questionnaire is Dr. Wilson's

Adrenal Fatigue Questionnaire that asks questions regarding:

- Key Signs and Symptoms (31)
- Energy Patterns (13)
- Frequently Observed Events (20 male; 22 female)
- Food Patterns (9)
- Aggravating Factors (10)
- Relieving Factors (4)

The questionnaire establishes both the total responses for the past and the present, and determines the severity of the condition. The questionnaire should, however, be done with a trained health practitioner who can effectively assess all the issues that might be involved and how to effectively deal with the issues.

EIGHT

Impact of Adrenal Fatigue on other Health Issues

Adrenal fatigue can be both the cause and the result of several other conditions. Unfortunately, conventional medicine is far too reductionist, meaning, they localize a symptom or condition to a given system, organ or cellular process.

Alternative health practitioners are not only more likely to look for the underlying issues, as opposed to simply try to manage the symptoms, but they will also look at the interactive issues. A good health practitioner will also want to address the concerns that will be able to resolve a number of issues simultaneously. For instance, improving glutathione levels addresses a wide range of issues. This will create a domino effect in a positive direction.

Another example is the mind-body interaction. Just as what is going on in the mind can have a huge impact on the body, what is happening in the body can have an impact on the mind. Different systems and substances affect both the brain and the body.

As noted in Chapter Two, the hypothalamus affects the pituitary, which affects the adrenal glands. This axis has an impact on a wide number of functions in the body:

- Digestion
- Energy storage and expenditure
- Immune system
- Mood and emotions
- Reactions to stress
- Sexuality
- Various body processes

Further, various processes that the body engages in, when suffering from chronic disease – from inflammatory disorders to heart disease to gut issues – place demands on your adrenal glands. Consequently, your adrenals should be attended to whether you are suffering from something as serious as a chronic disease or you simply wake up fatigued after a night's sleep.

Let us now look at some of the different conditions that evolve with, or are the result of, adrenal fatigue.

Alcoholism, Addiction and Adrenal Fatigue

Alcoholism, like any other disorder, can have a variety of causes. Many people believe it is strictly a psychological issue, and it certainly can be. People may start drinking to:

- Avoid family, relationship problems or work issues
- Avoid emotional conflict, either internal or external
- Cover up for feelings of inadequacy, not feeling loved, abandonment, etc.
- Fill a deep emotional void/hole
- Fit in or peer pressure

Or for a variety of other reasons.

Alcoholism may also be the result of:

- Poor self-discipline
- Making poor choices.

Did you know, though, that the development of alcoholism could be due to:

- Adrenal fatigue?
- Hypoglycemia (low blood sugar)?
- Pathogens in the liver or brain demanding nutrients?
- Magnesium deficiency?

For many people with addictions, the above

physiological issues are the driving cause rather than psychological issues.

For example, let's look at the effects of a magnesium deficiency.

Magnesium Deficiency

Magnesium is required for over 380 known basic cellular functions.

Here is a list of only some of the symptoms of magnesium deficiency:

Neurological Symptoms include:
Behavioural disturbances
Irritability
Anxiety
Lethargy
Impaired memory
Impaired cognitive function
Anorexia
Loss of appetite
Nausea and vomiting
Seizures

Metabolic Symptoms include:
Increased intracellular calcium
Hyperglycemia
Calcium deficiency
Potassium deficiency

Cardiovascular Symptoms include:
Irregular or rapid heartbeat
Coronary spasms

Muscular Symptoms include:
Impaired muscle coordination
Tremors
Involuntary eye movements and vertigo
Difficulty swallowing
Weakness
Muscle spasms
Tics
Muscle cramps
Hyperactive reflexes

In the case of children:
Growth retardation or "failure to thrive"

And in addition, we can also experience such diverse problems as:

- Depression
- Chronic fatigue syndrome
- ADHD
- Epilepsy
- Parkinson's disease
- Sleep problems
- Migraine
- Cluster headaches
- Osteoporosis
- Premenstrual syndrome
- Chest pain (angina)

- Cardiac arrhythmias
- Coronary artery disease and atherosclerosis
- Hypertension
- Type II diabetes
- Asthma

See:
http://www.ancient-minerals.com/magnesium-deficiency/symptoms-signs/#list

When we look at the stress response, we find that stress increases the production of the adrenal mineral corticoids, such as aldosterone. Aldosterone regulates the balance of minerals at the cellular level. Increased production of aldosterone promotes an increase in sodium retention (leading to high blood pressure) and a loss in magnesium and potassium. Just the low magnesium component alone can lead to all kinds of issues, including alcoholism and other addictions.

Hypoglycemia and adrenal fatigue can also run hand in hand with alcoholism and addiction. In fact, one of the classic signs of adrenal fatigue is hypoglycemia or low blood sugar.

Dr. Lam (MD, MPH, who runs an Adrenal Fatigue Center) claims that: In adrenal fatigue, the hypoglycemia experience is more often than not sub-clinical. This means that the person has clinical signs of hypoglycemia even though the blood plasma level is invariably above 60-70 mg/dl. Their fasting serum blood sugar and glucose tolerance tests are usually normal. Conventional doctors not aware of the adrenal influence will miss this.

See:
http://www.drlam.com/articles/adrenal_fatigue_and_hypoglycemia.asp

In fact, Dr. Lam claims that those with adrenal fatigue at Stage 3 and beyond require sugar replenishment every 2-3 hours.

How does this connect with addiction? Well, alcohol, carbohydrate or stimulant craving is often driven by the body's requirement for quick energy. This drive for sugar may result from a compromised adrenal function. Alcohol is a carbohydrate, more refined than table sugar, which promotes cells to generate energy quickly.

Of course, this sets off a sugar roller coaster ride that involves further adrenal and nutrients depletion. The alcohol consumption acts as a short-term compensation for the low adrenal function. At the same time, it also requires the adrenals to respond with the production of hormones to regulate both the energy production and the blood sugar balance, thus putting more of a strain on the already compromised adrenals.

Once this initial short-term "cover up" is gone, the adrenals are more depleted than ever. Now that the adrenals and nutrients are more depleted this leads to a hypoglycemia. The reaction is stronger than ever and the craving for the addiction, be it alcohol or something else, is even greater.

Allergies and Adrenal Fatigue

Like alcoholism and addictions, allergies can have a wide variety of causes. Allergies can be caused from:

- Metal toxicity
- POPs, PCBs, pesticides, herbicides, etc
- Low glutathione – required for development, response and regulation of immune cells – low glutathione can be the cause of a depletion of five different types of protein anti-bodies found in our immune system: IgA, IgM, IgG, IgD, and IgE; or the imbalance between different immune cells, for example, T1 and T2.
- Because 90% of our immune system resides in our gut – any gut dysfunction

can cause allergies:

- Inflammation
- Low pH
- Poor enzyme production
- Poor prebiotics
- Poor probiotics

Most allergies result in the increased release of histamine and other inflammatory-inducing substances. Consequently, the body needs to produce the necessary anti-inflammatory substances. Where do we find these?

One type comes from the adrenals in the form of cortisol. Yes, cortisol is a primary anti-inflammatory hormone. In fact, cortisol is responsible for regulating the inflammatory reactions in the body and thus, the adrenals play an important part in the role of allergies. But what if the adrenal glands are already compromised?

Again, we end up with a feedback cycle that works against us. If the adrenals are depleted and the body releases histamine, there is less cortisol to regulate the resulting inflammation so we experience an allergic reaction. The adrenals are then pushed even further to produce more cortisol in reaction, which depletes the adrenals even further.

Now we have even less cortisol available for the next situation, which can cause an even bigger reaction and can subsequently cause an even greater depletion in the adrenals.

Increased allergies also increase psychological stress, which also drains the adrenals. Do you not think addressing problems with the adrenals should be part of getting back to health?

Auto-immune system and Adrenal Fatigue

You probably know the drill by now. Yes, there are several causes of autoimmune dysfunction in the body. In general, with autoimmune dysfunction the white blood cells (immune cells) attack a given part of the body causing inflammation and creating various degrees of dysfunction.

As we know from above, the adrenal glands are responsible for secreting cortisol, an anti-inflammatory that regulates inflammation. However, if the adrenals are fatigued then the inflammation is not regulated and gets out of control. As a result, pharmaceutical companies created laboratory replications of the body's cortisol and use these drugs as:

- Anti-inflammatories
- Immunosuppressives

- Prevention of an Addisonian crisis
- Topically for skin rashes: eczema, psoriasis
- Injections for issues like gout

But these drugs have a long list of side effects. Unfortunately, the man made cortisol can have various detrimental effects on the body. The following is the short list of some of the major side effects produced by such drugs:

- Increased blood sugars for diabetics
- Emotional instability
  - Anxiety
  - Depression
  - Mania
  - Psychosis
  - Various psychiatric issues
- Difficulty concentrating
  - Mental confusion
  - Foggy thinking
  - Indecisiveness
- Weight gain
  - Increased appetite
- Facial swelling
  - Mouth sores
  - Dry mouth
- Fatigue and/or weakness
- Blurred vision

- Cataracts
- Glaucoma
- Abdominal pain
  - Black stools
  - Bloating
  - Diarrhea
- Painful hips and shoulders
  - Joint pain
  - Severe swelling
  - Leg pain and/or cramps
- Steroid induced osteoporosis and/or osteonecrosis
- Insomnia
- Stretch marks
- Fatty liver

See:
http://en.wikipedia.org/wiki/Prednisone#Side-effects
http://drugs.webmd.boots.com/drugs/drug-379-PREDNISOLONE.aspx?drugid=379&drugname=PREDNISOLONE&source=2&isTicTac=false
http://www.rheumatology.org.au/downloads/Prednisolone050910_000.pdf

Alternative medicine would suggest that it might be a lot wiser to start including anti-inflammatory foods and natural supplements in your diet; to support your adrenals and restore health, rather than take steroids to simply manage the symptoms, at cost to the rest of the body.

Burnout, Chronic Fatigue Syndrome and Adrenal Fatigue

We usually talk of burnout when we are discussing the work force. The term is loosely used when employees or executives are caught between demands and expectations from both above and below and can no longer achieve their required functions effectively.

It is also often applied to people caught in the middle at home, for instance, the mother who has to take care of both her children and her parents and go to work at the same time.

It can apply to the single mom who has to work and take care of the home and the children; who doesn't believe she has the right, nor can she find the time, to take care of herself.

Having to deal with these psychological stressors (both cognitive and emotional) take their toll on the adrenals. The following domino effect may start to occur (note, the sequence of events will be different for different people):

- Insulin resistance
- Metabolic syndrome
- Glucose intolerance
- High cortisol levels
- Hypertension
- Belly fat
- Atherosclerosis

If these conditions are not resolved, over a period of time, the resulting condition is adrenal fatigue. Typically, the adrenal fatigue does not happen overnight but there is a prolonged period of time wherein the issues begin to accumulate and the body compromises to accommodate, until finally the body just can't do it anymore. This results in:

- Increased cognitive impairment
  - Memory starts to deteriorate
  - Concentration starts to deteriorate
  - Indecisiveness increases
- Productivity starts to fail
- Emotional stability starts to waiver
  - Intolerance for others
  - Emotional outbursts
  - Stressed, overwhelmed
- Relationships start to suffer
  - People become more socially

withdrawn
- o   More impatient and less tolerant
- More reactivity rather than strategic thinking
  - o   People feel trapped and cornered without choices
  - o   People feel like they simply exist, putting in time, rather than living their lives.

Unless both the psychological and the physiological issues are taken care of, the downward spiral continues. The victims take more and more prescribed drugs and/or self-medicating substances while struggling to keep up, until ultimately they end up on stress leave.

Dental Health and Adrenal Fatigue

Now this is an interesting subject. Who would have thought that dental issues could be connected with adrenal fatigue? If we go to the Weston Price Foundation we find that they are connected.

Weston Price was a dentist who researched nutrition, dental work and their impact on the body between the 1920s and the 1930s.

Weston Price worked in conjunction with the Mayo Clinic and identified a number of connections between the teeth and the body that are not taught in Dental School *and* the types of pathogens that can be caught in these pathways that are not addressed in current dental practices. His research identified over 400 different types of bacteria in dental plaque that can cause a variety of issues from cardio issues to immune issues.

These include the following:

- Cracked teeth
- Decayed teeth
- Gingivitis
- Improperly extracted teeth
- Mercury fillings
- Refractory periodontitis
- Toxic Root canals
- Tooth abscesses

All of these can have an impact on the adrenals. Again, the inflammatory response caused by these bacteria cause the adrenals to produce a constant flow of cortisol to regulate the inflammation, thus depleting the adrenals.

We are all familiar with the fact that mercury, from mercury fillings in particular, has a deleterious impact on our immune system. In addition, it is specifically toxic to the adrenal glands and inhibits the adrenals from secreting hormones.

See:
http://www.drlam.com/articles/oral_health_and_vitamin_C.asp
http://www.adrenalfatigue.org/dental-health

Fibromyalgia and Adrenal Fatigue

There is a lot of controversy over the cause of fibromyalgia, probably because, like most other disorders and dysfunctions there is a wide number of causes.

For instance:

- Hormonal disturbances
- Chemical imbalances
- Stress induced disruption of the HPA
- Hereditary
- Neurotransmitter imbalance (serotonin and/or dopamine)
- Dis-regulated substance P (which amplifies pain signals)
- Low levels of human growth hormone
- Sleep disorders
- Viral infections
- Inflammatory disorders

See:
http://www.webmd.com/fibromyalgia/guide
/fibromyalgia-causes
http://www.adrenalfatigue.org/fibromyalgia

According to webMD.com, symptoms of fibromyalgia include:

- Chronic muscle pain, muscle spasms or tightness
- Moderate or severe fatigue and decreased energy
- Insomnia or waking up feeling just as tired as when you went to sleep
- Stiffness upon waking or after staying in one position for too long
- Difficulty remembering, concentrating, and performing simple mental tasks ("fibro fog")
- Abdominal pain, bloating, nausea, and constipation alternating with diarrhea (irritable bowel syndrome)
- Tension or migraine headaches
- Jaw and facial tenderness
- Sensitivity to one or more of the following: odors, noise, bright lights, medications, certain foods, and cold
- Feeling anxious or depressed
- Numbness or tingling in the face, arms, hands, legs, or feet
- Increase in urinary urgency or

frequency (irritable bladder)
- Reduced tolerance for exercise and muscle pain after exercise
- A feeling of swelling (without actual swelling) in the hands and feet

See: http://www.webmd.com/fibromyalgia/understanding-fibromyalgia-symptoms

As with many diagnoses there is a wide degree of overlap. Is fibromyalgia causing adrenal fatigue or is adrenal fatigue causing fibromyalgia? Can it go either way or are there common component(s) between the two of them?

Glutathione and Adrenal Fatigue

Another important nutrient involved in adrenal function is glutathione. Glutathione has long been recognized as the master anti-oxidant but in the last decade, it has been recognized for a lot more than its anti-oxidant functions.

Glutathione is a tripeptide that is made inside the cells. While we can take foods and supplemental glutathione, there are no transport mechanisms into the cells. So what do we do? First of all, let's understand the role of glutathione in the adrenal process.

To understand this process, we need to back up a step. Remember the HPA or the hypothalamic-pituitary-adrenal axis? Well, the CRH (corticotrophin-releasing hormone) is produced in the hypothalamus and "talks to" the pituitary. The pituitary then releases ACTH (adrenocorticotropic hormone) which signals the adrenal glands which then release cortisol. These substances are typically produced in response to biological stress.

Of course, there can be problems anywhere along this axis, but one of the problems we know of is when there is insufficient glutathione to make ACTH in the pituitary. *This means that the adrenals don't get told to respond.* Small wonder we have problems.

Research shows us that about 50 years ago, we used to lose about 1-2% of our levels of glutathione per year, from about the age of 20 onwards. Today, however, we are losing 12-15% per year and starting from younger and younger ages. Yes, we are depleted in glutathione!

We are significantly depleted in glutathione for a number of reasons. Glutathione is involved in all of the following processes:

- Anti-oxidant (master anti-oxidant – used in all categories of free radicals and

in all locations)
- Detoxification (both cellular and in the liver)
- Inflammation (important in effective resolution)
- Blood chelator (takes toxic metals out of our blood)
- Red blood cells (required for the uptake and release of oxygen and carbon dioxide)
- White blood cells (development, maintenance, response and regulatory balance)
- Hormone regulation
- Nitric oxide regulation (required for vaso-dilation or artery expansion)
- Protection of the mitochondria (produces the fuel for the cells)
- Protection and promotion of telomere synthesis and much more.

In today's society with overwhelming levels of toxicity (air, water and food) we can understand why we are so depleted in glutathione. If we add in the fact that we are undernourished and don't have the nutrients to make glutathione, we can understand another reason for our glutathione depletion.

If we don't have sufficient glutathione, we are not going to be able to produce ACTH. If we cannot produce ACTH, the adrenals are not told to get up and respond.

This is a big problem because what might be diagnosed as adrenal fatigue is really glutathione and ACTH depletion.

In Chapter Ten we will explore how we can improve glutathione levels and thus how to support the adrenal glands.

Herpes and Adrenal Fatigue

Most people who have herpes do not realize they have it. According to Common Health, more than 80% of those with herpes are undiagnosed. In fact, according to this article, Dr. Shier claimed that, "pretty much everyone gets it by the time they're elderly".

See:
http://commonhealth.wbur.org/2011/04/latest-genital-herpes

What does this have to do with adrenal fatigue? Well, the outbreak of herpes is known to increase with the following stressors:

- Corticosteroid use
- Strong emotions
- Illness
- Sunburn

- Trauma

If your immune system and your adrenals are strong, your body has a better capacity to deal with stressors. However, if your adrenals are fatigued, your immune system goes down and your capacity to fight herpes and/or herpes outbreak is greatly diminished.

Likewise, chronic outbreaks and chronic infections contribute to adrenal fatigue. Once again, we have a cycle that continues to go around and gets worse with each turn.

HIV, Hepatitis C and Adrenal Fatigue

Again we could have a circular situation going on here. Because of the interaction between the adrenals and the immune system, either one can predispose a person to the condition. However, we also know there is a variety of conditions with the liver that can predispose the liver to HIV and hepatitis. We also know that chronic conditions can provoke adrenal fatigue.

So regardless of which one leads the process, once you have HIV or Hepatitis, you should take care of the adrenals in order to support the body's capacity, and in particular the liver's capacity, to deal with the problem.

Hypoglycemia and Adrenal Fatigue

As noted earlier, hypoglycemia (low blood sugar) can be caused by stress but so can adrenal fatigue. Why is this? Stress, either gut or psychological, signals the body to release or generate an increase in blood sugars in order to generate energy to respond to the stress. The adrenals are then required to step up to the plate and increase the secretion of norepinephrine, epinephrine and cortisol in order to regulate the blood sugar levels.

Cortisol is utilized to create a temporary insulin resistance in the cells so that the cells are not overwhelmed with glucose and the body is not depleted too quickly of the blood glucose.

If the adrenals do not have the capacity to produce norepinephrine, epinephrine and cortisol then the cells get overwhelmed with the sugars and there is a drop in blood glucose levels. We call this condition hypoglycemia.

Prolonged stress or intermittent stress can cause sugar swings that aggravate hypoglycemic symptoms:

- intense hunger
- nervousness
- palpitations

- sweating
- trembling
- trouble speaking
- weakness

See:
http://www.medicinenet.com/hypoglycemia/page2.htm#toce

If the adrenals are fatigued, it becomes more and more difficult to regulate blood sugar levels. Thus, the reaction to stress becomes more and more depleting and the blood sugar levels are further depleted.

With low levels of epinephrine, norepinephrine and cortisol and a high level of sugar released into the system without regulation, the body cannot regulate the cell intake of glucose. While the cells require the glucose to make the energy, the over-production of glucose causes damage to the cells. Now the damaged cells need to be repaired or replaced but all this work requires energy, which requires glucose. During this process, the cells are becoming depleted in glucose and the nutrients required for other purposes.

The norepinephrine, epinephrine and cortisol help the liver convert glycogen (or stored sugar) and convert fats and carbohydrates into the glucose (gluconeogenesis) required for the energy production.

In order for the body to get its required sugars for energy, the body provokes a craving for sugar but at the same time you may also feel tired, weak and shaky.

If there is a simultaneous increase in insulin *and* decrease in norepinephrine, epinephrine, and cortisol, there is a rapid drop in blood sugar.

Typically, people will drink coffee or a soda to get their "energy" level back up. They will get an initial relief reaction as the sugar and/or caffeine hits them but the long-term effect of this short-term remedy is followed by even lower levels of blood sugar levels than they started with. So the roller coaster ride continues.

This is why people who experience chronic hypoglycemia are also typically experiencing adrenal fatigue. Likewise, people who have adrenal fatigue are also usually experiencing an irregular blood glucose pattern, typically hypoglycemia.

Unfortunately, if this cycle continues without interruption and a chance to bring the body back into balance, the person ends up becoming diabetic.

Typically, as a diabetic, the adrenals and the liver are not even addressed, just the insulin.

Immune System and Adrenal Fatigue

As noted above, the adrenals (and adrenal like hormones) are important components in the immune system function. They are involved when the immune system steps up to the plate to:

- Burn out pathogens with fever
- Carry out pathogens with mucus and sneezing
- Eliminate pathogens with diarrhea...

That's when inflammation occurs. The adrenals pump out the appropriate amount of cortisol to regulate the inflammatory response and the body comes back into balance.

So what happens if adrenal fatigue has begun? Magnesium and glutathione levels are now low. There is a greater experience of:

- Respiratory infections
  - Bronchitis
  - Pneumonia (Strep 50%, Pfeiffer's bacillus 20%, Chlamydophila pneumoniae 13%, Mycoplasma

pneumoniae 3%)
- Gut infections
  - shigellosis (caused by shigella)
  - salmonellosis (caused by salmonella)
  - parasitical infections
    - thread worm
    - amoebiasis (caused by amoebas)
    - giardiasis (caused by giardia)
- Allergic reactions
  - Environmental
  - Pharmaceutical
  - Food

The more severe the infection, the more frequently they happen, the more drugs taken for them, the more likely you are affecting your adrenal capacity to take care of you.

Just one episode can have prolonged detrimental effects depending on what is going on along concurrently. For instance, if you are already dealing with a difficult relationship or a stressful job, eating a nutrient-deficient diet (like most of North America) then the impact on your adrenals is going to be greater and they will take longer for recovery.

So, once again, we have to decide whether we are going to go for the short-term solution of taking anti-biotics with their long-term side effects or are we going to take care of the adrenals?

Mild Depression and Adrenal Fatigue

We have already explored how the side effects of many of the above issues involve cognitive and emotional dysfunction, so let's look at depression directly.

I worked as a psychologist for some twenty years and frequently referred people to other specialists. Typically in psychology we were taught that hypothyroid may be the cause of depression but psychologists are very limited in their understanding of how many other physical conditions can actually cause depression and other psychological disorders.

It only made sense that the brain requires a lot of nutrients to produce:

- Different types of Glial cells
    - Maintenance crew
    - Clean up crew
    - Recycling crews
    - Enzymes
- Neurons

- Neuro-hormones
- Neurotransmitters
- Structure
- Transport mechanisms

The brain would require a lot of different kinds of nutrients to support all of these different processes. I had to ask myself; what if there was disruption in how the nutrients got into the body, how the nutrients were metabolized and how the nutrients were transported to the brain?

So many things might affect the brain's capacity to function. Simply looking at how we interpret and respond to the world wasn't sufficient. As it turns out, that basic logic was right on.

We now know that the gut is responsible for the production of a vast amount of the body's neurotransmitters. For instance, the majority of the neurotransmitter that is usually associated with depression – serotonin, is made in the gut at 98%! Further, it is still a hypothesis that low serotonin even causes depression – despite the fact that the pharmaceutical companies bring in billions of dollars a day for different anti-depressants that have never been proven to resolve depression. In addition, these very anti-depressants that are supposed to take care of depression deplete the brain of the very nutrients required to make serotonin, which in turn leaves us dependent on the anti-depressants!

Getting back to the adrenals – what do the adrenals have to do with depression? Adrenal hormones are very involved in:

1) Cognitive function
2) Emotional experience and stability
3) The Hypothalamic – Pituitary – Adrenal Axis (HPA)

It makes perfect sense that the adrenals and depression (and other psychological issues) should be connected. If gut stress affects the adrenals and the gut and the adrenals produce neurotransmitters – then the brain is going to be affected if there is gut stress. Likewise if there are mental/emotional stresses and these kinds of stresses affect the adrenals, which produce neurotransmitters, there is going to be an impact on the brain. But don't forget, if the adrenals have an impact on the liver and the thyroid and each of these systems impact the brain – there is going to be an effect. These are just a few of the interactive dynamic processes.

Now don't forget, people can experience both a passive depression and an agitated depression. Can you guess how they are correlated with hyper- or hypo- adrenal activity?

The high cortisol and DHEA (Dehydroepian-drosterone) are associated with the agitated anxiety kind of depression, whereas the adrenal fatigue is associated with the more passive kind of depression. Yes it all makes sense so why isn't it utilized in either diagnostic processes or treatment processes?

DHEA is another substance made from cholesterol. It is the precursor for steroid hormones and produced by the adrenals.

In fact, DHEA has been shown to provoke a significant improvement in depression according to the Archives of General Psychiatry (2005, 62(2), p. 154 – 162).

PMS, Menopause and Adrenal Fatigue

Whereas the gonads and the pituitary both produce the sex hormones, only the adrenals produce testosterone in women. In addition, after menopause, the adrenals are the only source of the female hormones as well.

These hormones also play a role in:

1. Menstruation
2. PMS
3. Menopause

4. Sexual function

It is not surprising that women with adrenal fatigue also experience PMS, problems with perimenopause and menopause.

Throughout perimenopause, the ovaries decrease their production of the estrogens and progesterone. If the adrenals are fatigued they are unable to pick up the slack and create a smooth transition through menopause.

Unfortunately, if already compromised before menopause, the menopausal process may present a significant strain on the adrenals. Rather than providing artificial or bio-identical hormone therapy, which has provoked negative results and is extremely controversial, it might be easier and make more sense to support adrenal functioning.

Rheumatoid Arthritis and Adrenal Fatigue

As we have already noted, the adrenals play a role in both inflammatory processes and with the immune system. Thus, it is understandable that it has a role in Rheumatoid Arthritis (RA).

Like so many disorders, this painful inflammatory disease creates a cyclic effect. RA creates a chronic stress response in and of itself and therefore draws on the adrenals both for the anti-inflammatory cortisol and the stress response hormones thereby possibly creating fatigue, if it wasn't there before.

If this wasn't bad enough, the person often gets prescribed synthetic cortisols (corticosteroids) for the temporary relief of pain. The corticosteroids end up having a negative feedback impact on the production of cortisol from the adrenals, thus disabling the body's natural production of anti-inflammatories and immune regulation.

Unfortunately, it takes a long time for the adrenals to recover from corticosteroids.

Sleep and Adrenal Fatigue

We all know that sleep is a very important function. We actually do more work while sleeping than while awake. Most of the body's restorative functions occur while sleeping.

Like most organs in the body, the adrenals go through their own cycles during the 24-hour cycle (circadian rhythm). Cortisol production is highest around 8 a.m. and lowest after midnight (until about 4 a.m.).

Unfortunately, both high and low levels of cortisol can interrupt sleep. Both chronic and acute stress can provoke surges in the HPA, which can have a negative impact on sleep causing:

- Longer time getting to sleep
- Sleep fragmentation
- Decreased slow-wave sleep
- Shortened sleep times

In typical feedback style, sleep disturbances can provoke further HPA dysfunction.

As we have already noted, prolonged hyper-adrenal functioning eventually leads to adrenal fatigue. With adrenal fatigue we have low blood sugar, which also causes sleep disruption. Normally we have a low blood glucose in the morning hours but with adrenal fatigue and even lower blood glucose levels, the body's internal system wakes the person up in order to get more nutrient, and in particular, glucose into the body.

Chronic insomnia can, in and of itself, lead to a variety of health issues:

- Impaired cognitive functioning
- Elevated estrogen levels
- Impaired glucose tolerance
- Impaired hormonal regulation
- Increased carbohydrate/sugar cravings

- Low AM cortisol levels
- Lowered immunity
- Slow healing processes

Weight gain and Adrenal Fatigue

We now know the production of cortisol from the adrenal gland helps to regulate insulin but there is another hormone that is also involved in food metabolism called leptin. Leptin plays an important role in:

- the maintenance of energy balance
- thermogenesis
- energy expenditure
- perception of hunger and appetite
- metabolism
- the hypothalamic-pituitary-adrenal axis.

We know that cortisol is an inflammatory regulator and an insulin regulator. Without the control on inflammation, the liver begins to make an acute phase inflammatory protein called CRP (C-Reactive Protein). In addition, inflammation causes leptin resistance (which impacts on energy production in the body).

Inflammation and adrenal dysfunction both cause interference in the thyroid hormones T4 –T3 conversion that occurs in the liver which has a further impact on the cells' metabolic activity.

These different processes each have their own domino effect. All of these issues converge on the body's development of weight issues.

So focusing on calories and metabolism are only two very simple components of a very complex program (and we have only touched on a few of the components that contribute to weight gain).

NINE

Resolving Adrenal Fatigue

Can people experiencing adrenal fatigue feel their best again?

Yes, they can.

Unfortunately, it takes a lot longer to help the adrenals return to normal functioning than it does the liver. With the liver, we can detoxify and strengthen in relatively short periods of time. It has one of the highest turnover rates, if you will, of any organ in the body.

However, the adrenals take considerably longer than the liver to regenerate and produce in an effective and healthy way, but it *is* possible to regain health. With effective care most people experiencing adrenal fatigue can expect to feel good again.

There are two primary tricks to being able the adrenals:

- Recognize that the problem you have is, in fact, adrenal related.
- Finding a good health practitioner with whom to work.

Dr. Wilson is a practitioner well known for his adrenal fatigue program. As most alternative physicians would suggest there are a number of aspects of life that need to be dealt with. These include:

- Lifestyle – finding/creating a lifestyle that does not provoke cognitive or emotional stress.
- Diet – working with an organic high-nutrient diet that provides the nutrients the body requires to heal itself.
- Herbal medicine is also well known for its capacity to work with the adrenals – there are many herbs that strengthen the adrenals in different ways, if used wisely.
- Mind-body interaction – finding techniques that allow both the mind and the body to calm down, relax and regenerate.

Let's go through each of these individually.

Lifestyle

How can you possibly expect the adrenals to regenerate and heal if you continue to function in a stressed out, conflicted, toxic environment?

Perhaps you need to take a stress leave, get out

of a bad relationship, take a prolonged holiday or leave a stressful job. You know the situation you are in and ultimately, you know what you need to do.

The problem with this kind of reasoning is that people often stay in these situations because of two reasons: fear and feeling trapped. I have provided a short list of issues and a few examples of each.

1) Fear: There are many underlying situations that can provoke fear and many of them have blurry boundaries so the situation becomes complicated.
2) Fear of the unknown: Thinking that the devil you know is better than the devil you don't know.
   - Staying with a verbally abusive husband is better than finding another that may be physically abusive, etc.
   - Staying married is better than being single.
3) Fear of unknown possible consequences:
   - Might have to work harder.
   - Might have to learn how to do something else.
   - Perception that having once made a decision, you cannot make other choices.
4) Fear of not being able to handle or cope

with the situation involved in the transition or the outcome:

- Being able to handle the emotional upheaval.
- Being able to work two jobs.
- Being able to get the grades.

5) Fear of other people's perceptions and/or pressure:

- People will think I am a failure.
- People will tell me to go back.
- People will tell me I am wrong.

6) Fear of your own inadequacies being recognized:

- People will find out that I am not good enough.
- People will find out who I really am.
- People will hate me.

7) Fear of success and likewise fear of failure:

- Fear of taking responsibility for your actions.
- Fear of having people expect more of you.
- Fear of having to make other choices/decisions down the road.

8) Fear of pain (spiritual, emotional, or physical):

- Fear of conflict internally: beliefs, morals, values, etc.
- Fear of physical pain being imposed on you: accident, an abuser, etc.

9) Trapped: Feeling trapped is a perception –

ultimately we all have choices; some have better probabilities than others; some we are more willing to tackle than others.

Ultimately, feeling trapped is the result of not believing you have a choice.

1. Trapped in a job/career situation
    - because of finances
    - because of time restrictions
    - because of family pressure
    - because of self imposed pressure
2. Trapped in a marriage
    - because of finances
    - because of children
    - because of peers, social pressure, social facade
    - because of guilt, shame or inadequacy
3. Trapped in a family dynamic
    - don't want to bring shame to the family
    - don't want to cause a ripple
    - guilt and/or shame keep you silent
4. Trapped by your own moral dilemma or value system
    - children come first
    - family comes first
    - you made your bed, now lie in it
5. Trapped by your belief system
    - keep going regardless of how you

feel
- strong work ethic
- stiff upper lip

If any of these possibilities is causing stress in your life, the adrenals are going to suffer. Even when we provide proper nutrition, diet and exercise, if we persist in engaging in the underlying problems causing the stress then our attempts at resolving the problem are going to be weak.

Diet

Let's now look at some of the other types of lifestyle issues that can also play a part:

- Diet
- Exercise
- Addiction

Diet and exercise are big issues in North America. It is well recognized that in North America we are overfed and undernourished. Why? Because our food is:

- Genetically modified
- Processed
- Pasteurized
- Microwaved
- Laboratory generated

- Toxic with POPs, PCBs, pesticides, herbicides, growth hormones, antibiotics, and more.

Also, the ground in which we grow the food is too often barren of minerals and nutrients because it has been over farmed and underfed.

Our bodies require good nutrient. If we are not willing to alter our diet, to provide good healthy nutrients then how is the body expected to recover?

Vitamin C

Vitamin C is an important nutrient component when dealing with the adrenals. The highest concentrations of Vitamin C are in the:

- Eyes
- Brain
- Adrenal glands

Stress, infection and heavy duty exercise all require increases in Vitamin C. The production of cortisol and the other adrenal hormones are dependent on Vitamin C. Therefore, if the supply of nutrients is low, so is the production of these substances.

While most animals can produce their own Vitamin C, human beings cannot. We are missing the last enzyme in the process. At least we can get this from food and supplementation. Consequently, it is called an essential vitamin. Foods known for their high Vitamin C content are:

- Red and green hot chili peppers
- Guavas
- Bell peppers
- Herbs, like parsley and thyme
- Broccoli, cauliflower and Brussels sprouts
- Kiwi fruit
- Papayas
- Oranges and tangerines
- Strawberries

If we are healthy, then it is suggested that we require approximately 500-1000mg of Vitamin C daily. However, if we are suffering from adrenal fatigue, Dr. Wilson (author of: Adrenal Fatigue: The 21st Century Stress Syndrome) claims that these people may need up to 20,000 mg!

The bowel tolerance test is the most common Vitamin C test. While this is also used for other nutrients like magnesium, it is effective. Here is how it works: One keeps taking increasingly higher doses of Vitamin C until they get three days of lose bowels. When that happens, start reducing the amounts. The controversial argument around this method is that it may reflect tolerance as opposed to optimum requirements.

Finally, when working with Vitamin C it's important to know if not to use man-made Vitamin C as it is simply a synthetic version of the outer ring of Vitamin C. As such, it lacks all of the naturally occurring bioflavonoids, enzymes, hormones and other phytonutrients that are part of the complex substance and thus requires the body's nutrients to help metabolize it thus causing other nutritional deficiencies.

Glutathione

There are two major ways to increase the production of glutathione in the body:

1) We need to make sure the DNA responsible for the glutathione production tools are turned on. Dr. McCord's 5 herb formulation called Protandim, is known to do this through the Nrf2 pathways. Note, there are several pathways that compounds can maneuver through the cellular processes. From the ECM (the extra cellular matrix) that provides structural support for cells – through the membrane of the cell and the membrane

transport systems into the cell – through the internal cellular transport systems. The Nrf2 is a pathway that is known to connect and impact on the nucleus of the cell and the actual DNA.

Studied in over twenty universities with fantastic results, Protandim is not only known for turning on the tools to make glutathione but is also known to turn on these other pathways:

a. Anti-inflammatory
b. Anti-oxidant
   i. Glutathione
   ii. SOD (super oxide dismutases)
   iii. Catalases
c. Anti-fibrosis

2) Provide the nutrients for the cells to make glutathione. Thanks to Dr. Keller's work we have a formulation of all the nutrients in the right ratios that provide the body with a "pancake mix", so to speak, of what the cells require to make glutathione.

Thus, we now have the ability to both turn on the tools and provide the nutrients to increase the glutathione levels thus enabling the production of ACTH in the pituitary, which in turn tells the adrenals to respond.

Vitamin B complex

In some cases, like in the earlier stages of adrenal issues, you'd want to use more DHEA and less pregnenolone because cortisol levels are high. Cortisol is catabolic and DHEA is anabolic, so you want the increased amount of DHEA to balance out the catabolic effects of cortisol. But DHEA can antagonize cortisol, so if you're in the later stage of adrenal fatigue where cortisol is really low and you take a bunch of DHEA, that could actually make things worse.

If you're going to use sublingual hormones like pregnenolone and DHEA, make sure you know what you're doing or that you're working with somebody that does. If you're using therapeutic-strength adaptogens in a liquid extract formula or something, I still recommend that you work with a good herbalist, but if you're just taking formulas like Adaptocrine or Adrenotone, I think it's pretty safe to do that on your own.

In addition, we may have to add extra to the diet, for instance good adrenal herbs and supplements. These herbs are called adatogenic because they help the whole body deal with and recover from stress more effectively, predominantly because of their impact on the adrenal glands.

The following are some examples of good adrenal herbs that are utilized, however, it is important to work with someone who understands which ones are used to:

- raise cortisol
- reduce cortisol
- strengthen the adrenals

In addition, some should be utilized together, whereas other should be utilized solo.

- Ginseng:
  - Gynostemma pentaphyllum
  - Eleutherococcus
  - Panax
  - Ashwagandha
- Schizandra
- Rhodiola
- Licorice (not typically used if there is a cardio situation).

There are other modalities as well, they may also benefit the body, but are beyond the scope of this book:

- Ayurvedic detox and massage and diet
- Traditional Chinese Medicine acupuncture, herbs and diet

- Homeopathic remedies

In addition, you may need to engage in a different form of exercise. For instance, if you have a gym/workout addiction, you may have to tone down your exercise regimen to allow the adrenals to heal.

Conversely, if you tend to avoid exercise, you may have to get into a regimen to help move the fluids, blood, lymph, etc. around the body so that the body can detoxify and get nutrients to and from all the different tissues.

Leaky gut resolution

If you have leaky gut, there are many things you can do to help heal your intestinal epithelium. First, identify and eliminate any foods that may be contributing to the problem. (See my earlier blogs on making sense of food allergies, identifying food allergies, and eliminating food allergies and sensitivities for more on problematic foods). Then, utilize nutrients that can support repair of the tissue. Glutamine is the primary fuel for intestinal cells. It preserves intestinal structure and maintains healthy permeability. Quercetin, a flavonoid, also supports intestinal barrier function. Both L-glycine and phosphatidylcholine help to support normal levels of inflammation. Nutrients such as vitamin A, vitamin C, and zinc enhance intestinal repair and function.

Stress impacts many different conditions through its damaging effects on the gut. By supporting your gut, you may be able to improve your health in a multitude of other areas as well.

Dr. Wilson's Adrenal Fatigue Supplement Program

Dr. Wilson's Adrenal Fatigue Supplement Program combines suggestions about lifestyle, diet, rest and body-mind techniques with specific recommendations for dietary supplementation. Together they create a comprehensive Program for Adrenal Fatigue and Stress that effectively supports and promotes healthy adrenal function, vitality and stress hardiness.

We have found that one of the easiest ways to quickly see if adrenal fatigue may be affecting you is to look at the cartoons that begin on page 27 in Dr. Wilson's book *Adrenal Fatigue: The 21st Century Stress Syndrome*. If three or more of the cartoons remind you of yourself, complete the self-grading Adrenal Fatigue Questionnaire on page 61 in the book.

Read the dietary and lifestyle suggestions found in Chapter 12 and Chapter 13 of the book and use the information to start making changes in your life that will support your body and your ability to handle stress. Many of these changes should be for life. Do the ones that are easiest for you to change first.

Sometimes even little changes can make a surprising difference. Work up to the ones that are more challenging and go at a pace that doesn't stress you more. If you are feeling very overwhelmed, it can help to take a long-term perspective and realize that if you keep gradually improving your life one step at a time, you will get there. In six months, a year, two years you will be able to look back and see that you really have come a long way from where you are now. Many people have shared this journey and are very glad they did.

Dr. Wilson designed the four supplements in the Adrenal Fatigue Quartet® to work together to promote this process of revitalization and enhance your stress resilience.* The directions below are based on Dr. Wilson's clinical experience with what produces optimal results. They work deeply with your body's own health-building processes, so it is important to give yourself enough time to experience a lasting difference. We recommend you continue using them as suggested for a minimum of six months to two years. Let how you feel guide you.

Click on the directions below to see the recommended supplement schedule using the Doctor Wilson's Original Formulations adrenal supplements: Adrenal C Formula, Adrenal Rebuilder, Super Adrenal Stress Formula and Herbal Adrenal Support Formula (or it's alternate Herbal HPA).

- Mild Adrenal Fatigue
- Moderate Adrenal Fatigue
- Severe Adrenal Fatigue

http://www.adrenalfatigue.org/program-for-adrenal-fatigue-stress

References:
http://blog.adrenalfatigue.org/digestive-health/stress-and-leaky-gut-implications-and-solutions/

http://drlwilson.com/articles/allergies.htm

http://en.wikipedia.org/wiki/Hypothalamic%E2%80%93pituitary%E2%80%93adrenal_axis
http://naturalmedicinejournal.net/pdf/NMJ_JUNE10_TC.pdf

http://raphaelkellmanmd.com/health-issues-we-treat/stress-and-adrenal-fatigue/
http://robbwolf.com/2012/04/09/real-deal-adrenal-fatigue/

http://www.adrenalfatiguefocus.org/adaptogenic-herbs-in-adrenal-fatigue.html

http://www.adrenalfatigue.org/what-is-adrenal-fatigue#what-is-adrenal-fatigue

http://www.drlam.com/articles/adrenal_fatigue_and_hypoglycemia.asp

http://www.medicinenet.com/allergy/page2.htm#what_causes_allergies

http://www.prohealth.com/me-cfs/blog/boardDetail.cfm?id=1054627
http://www.tvernonlac.com/

Websites for nutritional data:
http://www.healthaliciousness.com/nutritionfacts/nutrition-comparison.php?o=11233&t=11270&h=11203&s=67.00&e=56.00&r=50.00
http://www.healthaliciousness.com/articles/

Books:

Dr. Wilson's book, *Adrenal Fatigue: The 21st Century Stress Syndrome*

Dr. Wilson's book *Adrenal Fatigue: The 21st Century Stress Syndrome* and check out Dr. Wilson's Health Tips and his Program for Adrenal Fatigue and Stress on this website.

For more information, consult Dr. Wilson's book, *Adrenal Fatigue: The 21st Century Stress Syndrome*. It contains a wealth of insights and a series of tests you can do at home, as well as lab tests like the saliva test for adrenal hormones to help you determine if you are experiencing adrenal fatigue.* Also see Could I be experiencing adrenal fatigue?

Fox C, Ramsoomair D, Carter C. Magnesium: its proven and potential clinical significance.

SOUTHERN MEDICAL JOURNAL. 2003;94(12):1195-201. Available at: http://www.medscape.com/viewarticle/4235 68_1. Accessed March 8, 2010